I0091392

Gratitude Journal

I am Grateful for

Monday _____
_____
_____
_____

Tuesday _____
_____
_____
_____

Wednesday _____
_____
_____
_____

Thursday _____
_____
_____
_____

I am Grateful for

Friday _____

_____

_____

_____

_____

Saturday _____

_____

_____

_____

_____

Sunday _____

_____

_____

_____

By releasing expectation and embracing gratitude we become happier.

I am Grateful for

Monday _____
_____
_____
_____

Tuesday _____
_____
_____
_____

Wednesday _____
_____
_____
_____
_____

Thursday _____
_____
_____
_____
_____

I am Grateful for

Friday _____

_____

_____

_____

Saturday _____

_____

_____

_____

_____

Sunday _____

_____

_____

_____

Forgiveness is a gift to ourselves not to another, freeing us from the past and opening a gate to a more positive future.

I am Grateful for

Monday _____
_____
_____
_____

Tuesday _____
_____
_____
_____

Wednesday _____
_____
_____
_____

Thursday _____
_____
_____
_____

I am Grateful for

Friday _____
_____
_____
_____
_____

Saturday _____
_____
_____
_____
_____

Sunday _____
_____
_____
_____

When you choose to open yourself up to love, you embrace life at its highest potential.

I am Grateful for

Monday _____

_____

_____

_____

Tuesday _____

_____

_____

_____

Wednesday _____

_____

_____

_____

_____

Thursday _____

_____

_____

_____

_____

I am Grateful for

Friday _____
_____
_____
_____

Saturday _____
_____
_____
_____
_____

Sunday _____
_____
_____
_____

Gratitude harmonises our inner core.

I am Grateful for

Monday _____
_____
_____
_____

Tuesday _____
_____
_____
_____

Wednesday _____
_____
_____
_____

Thursday _____
_____
_____
_____

I am Grateful for

Friday _____

_____

_____

_____

Saturday _____

_____

_____

_____

_____

Sunday _____

_____

_____

_____

Being humble is not a weakness;
it shows strength of character

I am Grateful for

Monday _____
_____
_____
_____

Tuesday _____
_____
_____
_____

Wednesday _____
_____
_____
_____
_____

Thursday _____
_____
_____
_____
_____

I am Grateful for

Friday _____
_____
_____
_____
_____

Saturday _____
_____
_____
_____
_____
_____

Sunday _____
_____
_____
_____

When we choose to give unconditionally,
we receive so much in return.

I am Grateful for

Monday _____

_____

_____

_____

Tuesday _____

_____

_____

_____

Wednesday _____

_____

_____

_____

Thursday _____

_____

_____

_____

I am Grateful for

Friday _____

_____

_____

_____

Saturday _____

_____

_____

_____

_____

Sunday _____

_____

_____

_____

A good deed can have a snowball effect;
it has the potential to change the world.

I am Grateful for

Monday _____
_____
_____
_____

Tuesday _____
_____
_____
_____

Wednesday _____
_____
_____
_____
_____

Thursday _____
_____
_____
_____

I am Grateful for

Friday _____

_____

_____

_____

Saturday _____

_____

_____

_____

_____

Sunday _____

_____

_____

_____

By being true to your personal aspirations,
you gift yourself your best possible life.

I am Grateful for

Monday _____

_____

_____

_____

Tuesday _____

_____

_____

_____

Wednesday _____

_____

_____

_____

Thursday _____

_____

_____

_____

I am Grateful for

Friday _____

_____

_____

_____

_____

Saturday _____

_____

_____

_____

_____

Sunday _____

_____

_____

_____

Our intention has a lot to do with
the response we receive.

I am Grateful for

Monday _____

_____

_____

_____

Tuesday _____

_____

_____

_____

Wednesday _____

_____

_____

_____

Thursday _____

_____

_____

_____

I am Grateful for

Friday _____

_____

_____

_____

Saturday _____

_____

_____

_____

_____

Sunday _____

_____

_____

_____

Inspiration is often the first step along
an exciting journey of creation.

I am Grateful for

Monday _____

_____

_____

_____

Tuesday _____

_____

_____

_____

Wednesday _____

_____

_____

_____

Thursday _____

_____

_____

_____

I am Grateful for

Friday _____

_____

_____

_____

Saturday _____

_____

_____

_____

Sunday _____

_____

_____

_____

Laughter is a cure to many ailments.
Find time to laugh every day.

I am Grateful for

Monday _____

_____

_____

_____

Tuesday _____

_____

_____

_____

Wednesday _____

_____

_____

_____

_____

Thursday _____

_____

_____

_____

_____

I am Grateful for

Friday _____

_____

_____

_____

_____

Saturday _____

_____

_____

_____

_____

Sunday _____

_____

_____

_____

Listen to your inner guide.
It has your best interest at heart.

I am Grateful for

Monday _____

_____

_____

_____

Tuesday _____

_____

_____

_____

Wednesday _____

_____

_____

_____

Thursday _____

_____

_____

_____

I am Grateful for

Friday _____
_____
_____
_____
_____

Saturday _____
_____
_____
_____
_____

Sunday _____
_____
_____
_____

Approach difficulties with a loving perspective and they will be resolved easier.

I am Grateful for

Monday _____
_____
_____
_____

Tuesday _____
_____
_____
_____

Wednesday _____
_____
_____
_____
_____

Thursday _____
_____
_____
_____
_____

I am Grateful for

Friday _____

_____

_____

_____

_____

Saturday _____

_____

_____

_____

_____

Sunday _____

_____

_____

_____

Happiness is a treasure we all have buried inside.

I am Grateful for

Monday _____
_____
_____
_____

Tuesday _____
_____
_____
_____

Wednesday _____
_____
_____
_____

Thursday _____
_____
_____
_____

I am Grateful for

Friday _____
_____
_____
_____
_____

Saturday _____
_____
_____
_____
_____

Sunday _____
_____
_____
_____

Everyone we connect with helps us to learn more about ourselves. We learn the most from those we disagree with.

I am Grateful for

Monday _____
_____
_____
_____

Tuesday _____
_____
_____
_____

Wednesday _____
_____
_____
_____
_____

Thursday _____
_____
_____
_____

I am Grateful for

Friday _____

_____

_____

_____

_____

Saturday _____

_____

_____

_____

_____

Sunday _____

_____

_____

_____

Our feelings indicate who we are and highlight the areas of ourselves that we can work on to grow stronger.

I am Grateful for

Monday _____

_____

_____

_____

Tuesday _____

_____

_____

_____

Wednesday _____

_____

_____

_____

Thursday _____

_____

_____

_____

I am Grateful for

Friday _____

_____

_____

_____

_____

Saturday _____

_____

_____

_____

_____

Sunday _____

_____

_____

_____

Positive thinking helps us to maintain a
healthy mind, body and spirit.

I am Grateful for

Monday _____
_____
_____
_____

Tuesday _____
_____
_____
_____

Wednesday _____
_____
_____
_____

Thursday _____
_____
_____
_____

I am Grateful for

Friday _____

_____

_____

_____

_____

Saturday _____

_____

_____

_____

_____

Sunday _____

_____

_____

_____

Even the happiest people
have low moments.

I am Grateful for

Monday _____

_____

_____

_____

Tuesday _____

_____

_____

_____

Wednesday _____

_____

_____

_____

Thursday _____

_____

_____

_____

I am Grateful for

Friday _____

_____

_____

_____

_____

Saturday _____

_____

_____

_____

_____

Sunday _____

_____

_____

_____

Aspire to be your best;
not someone else's.

I am Grateful for

Monday _____

_____

_____

_____

Tuesday _____

_____

_____

_____

Wednesday _____

_____

_____

_____

Thursday _____

_____

_____

_____

I am Grateful for

Friday _____

_____

_____

_____

_____

Saturday _____

_____

_____

_____

_____

Sunday _____

_____

_____

_____

Gratitude
is a divine characteristic.

I am Grateful for

Monday _____

_____

_____

_____

Tuesday _____

_____

_____

_____

Wednesday _____

_____

_____

_____

_____

Thursday _____

_____

_____

_____

_____

I am Grateful for

Friday _____

_____

_____

_____

_____

Saturday _____

_____

_____

_____

_____

Sunday _____

_____

_____

_____

When we combine our thoughts and
wishes with those of another,
magic happens.

I am Grateful for

Monday _____

_____

_____

_____

_____

Tuesday _____

_____

_____

_____

_____

Wednesday _____

_____

_____

_____

_____

Thursday _____

_____

_____

_____

_____

I am Grateful for

Friday _____
_____
_____
_____
_____

Saturday _____
_____
_____
_____
_____

Sunday _____
_____
_____
_____

Love gives us a special glow that everyone can see shine.

I am Grateful for

Monday _____

_____

_____

_____

_____

Tuesday _____

_____

_____

_____

_____

Wednesday _____

_____

_____

_____

_____

_____

Thursday _____

_____

_____

_____

_____

I am Grateful for

Friday _____

_____

_____

_____

_____

Saturday _____

_____

_____

_____

_____

Sunday _____

_____

_____

_____

You will never be alone when you discover self-love.

I am Grateful for

Monday _____

_____

_____

_____

_____

Tuesday _____

_____

_____

_____

_____

Wednesday _____

_____

_____

_____

_____

Thursday _____

_____

_____

_____

_____

I am Grateful for

Friday _____
_____
_____
_____
_____

Saturday _____
_____
_____
_____
_____

Sunday _____
_____
_____
_____

We have already lived in our past and not yet in our future.

What do you choose to focus most on?

I am Grateful for

Monday _____

_____

_____

_____

Tuesday _____

_____

_____

_____

Wednesday _____

_____

_____

_____

_____

Thursday _____

_____

_____

_____

I am Grateful for

Friday _____

_____

_____

_____

Saturday _____

_____

_____

_____

_____

Sunday _____

_____

_____

_____

Happiness
is in the heart of the beholder

I am Grateful for

Monday _____

_____

_____

_____

Tuesday _____

_____

_____

_____

Wednesday _____

_____

_____

_____

_____

Thursday _____

_____

_____

_____

I am Grateful for

Friday _____

_____

_____

_____

_____

Saturday _____

_____

_____

_____

_____

Sunday _____

_____

_____

_____

A butterfly already knows what it is like to
be a caterpillar; but a caterpillar can only trust
that it is worth the effort to become a butterfly.

I am Grateful for

Monday _____
_____
_____
_____

Tuesday _____
_____
_____
_____

Wednesday _____
_____
_____
_____

Thursday _____
_____
_____
_____

I am Grateful for

Friday _____

_____

_____

_____

_____

Saturday _____

_____

_____

_____

_____

Sunday _____

_____

_____

_____

We can make a difference where we are right now. By making one positive difference in our lives that touches the heart of another,

we have started a chain reaction.

I am Grateful for

Monday _____

_____

_____

_____

Tuesday _____

_____

_____

_____

Wednesday _____

_____

_____

_____

_____

Thursday _____

_____

_____

_____

I am Grateful for

Friday _____

_____

_____

_____

_____

Saturday _____

_____

_____

_____

_____

Sunday _____

_____

_____

_____

Take some quiet time out to get to
know your best friend who will never
ever let you down. yourself!

I am Grateful for

Monday _____

_____

_____

_____

Tuesday _____

_____

_____

_____

Wednesday _____

_____

_____

_____

_____

Thursday _____

_____

_____

_____

_____

I am Grateful for

Friday _____

_____

_____

_____

_____

Saturday _____

_____

_____

_____

_____

_____

Sunday _____

_____

_____

_____

Take a moment to consider an element of life
that you have not explored before.

You may be amazed at what you discover.

I am Grateful for

Monday _____
_____
_____
_____
_____

Tuesday _____
_____
_____
_____
_____

Wednesday _____
_____
_____
_____
_____

Thursday _____
_____
_____
_____
_____

I am Grateful for

Friday _____

_____

_____

_____

Saturday _____

_____

_____

_____

_____

Sunday _____

_____

_____

_____

Honesty
frees us from the shadows of secrecy.

I am Grateful for

Monday _____

_____

_____

_____

Tuesday _____

_____

_____

_____

Wednesday _____

_____

_____

_____

_____

Thursday _____

_____

_____

_____

_____

I am Grateful for

Friday _____

_____

_____

_____

_____

Saturday _____

_____

_____

_____

_____

Sunday _____

_____

_____

_____

We all have something special
and individual to offer the world.

I am Grateful for

Monday _____

_____

_____

_____

Tuesday _____

_____

_____

_____

Wednesday _____

_____

_____

_____

_____

Thursday _____

_____

_____

_____

_____

I am Grateful for

Friday _____
_____
_____
_____

Saturday _____
_____
_____
_____
_____

Sunday _____
_____
_____
_____

Awareness of our surroundings and interactions helps us to maximise the potential of each moment

I am Grateful for

Monday _____
_____
_____
_____

Tuesday _____
_____
_____
_____

Wednesday _____
_____
_____
_____

Thursday _____
_____
_____
_____

I am Grateful for

Friday _____
_____
_____
_____
_____

Saturday _____
_____
_____
_____
_____

Sunday _____
_____
_____
_____

Our energy is what people
remember when they encounter us.

I am Grateful for

Monday _____
_____
_____
_____
_____

Tuesday _____
_____
_____
_____
_____

Wednesday _____
_____
_____
_____
_____

Thursday _____
_____
_____
_____
_____

I am Grateful for

Friday _____

_____

_____

_____

_____

Saturday _____

_____

_____

_____

_____

Sunday _____

_____

_____

_____

A treasured gift that we can give to our self or another is the gift of Belief!

It helps us grow.

I am Grateful for

Monday _____

_____

_____

_____

Tuesday _____

_____

_____

_____

Wednesday _____

_____

_____

_____

_____

Thursday _____

_____

_____

_____

I am Grateful for

Friday _____
_____
_____
_____
_____

Saturday _____
_____
_____
_____
_____

Sunday _____
_____
_____
_____

What is the true meaning of life?
It is whatever you choose it to be.

I am Grateful for

Monday _____

_____

_____

_____

Tuesday _____

_____

_____

_____

Wednesday _____

_____

_____

_____

Thursday _____

_____

_____

_____

I am Grateful for

Friday _____

_____

_____

_____

_____

Saturday _____

_____

_____

_____

_____

Sunday _____

_____

_____

_____

Hope
is an important ingredient of life.

I am Grateful for

Monday _____
_____
_____
_____

Tuesday _____
_____
_____
_____

Wednesday _____
_____
_____
_____
_____

Thursday _____
_____
_____
_____

I am Grateful for

Friday _____
_____
_____
_____

Saturday _____
_____
_____
_____
_____

Sunday _____
_____
_____
_____

Share a smile with a stranger;
it may make a difference to their day.

I am Grateful for

Monday _____

_____

_____

_____

_____

Tuesday _____

_____

_____

_____

_____

Wednesday _____

_____

_____

_____

_____

Thursday _____

_____

_____

_____

_____

I am Grateful for

Friday _____

_____

_____

_____

_____

Saturday _____

_____

_____

_____

_____

Sunday _____

_____

_____

_____

Have faith that in honoring your
intentions you are being true to yourself.

I am Grateful for

Monday _____

_____

_____

_____

Tuesday _____

_____

_____

_____

Wednesday _____

_____

_____

_____

Thursday _____

_____

_____

_____

I am Grateful for

Friday _____

_____

_____

_____

_____

Saturday _____

_____

_____

_____

_____

Sunday _____

_____

_____

_____

Connect with the peripheral world;
do this by opening your mind
to the wider picture.

I am Grateful for

Monday _____

_____

_____

_____

_____

Tuesday _____

_____

_____

_____

_____

Wednesday _____

_____

_____

_____

_____

Thursday _____

_____

_____

_____

_____

I am Grateful for

Friday _____

_____

_____

_____

_____

Saturday _____

_____

_____

_____

_____

Sunday _____

_____

_____

_____

Change is something to embrace, not to
fear. It helps us live our best life,
learn and achieve our dreams.

I am Grateful for

Monday _____
_____
_____
_____

Tuesday _____
_____
_____
_____

Wednesday _____
_____
_____
_____

Thuursday _____
_____
_____
_____

I am Grateful for

Friday _____

_____

_____

_____

Saturday _____

_____

_____

_____

_____

Sunday _____

_____

_____

_____

Being grateful is to recognise the
Love in everything we receivE.

I am Grateful for

Monday _____

_____

_____

_____

Tuesday _____

_____

_____

_____

Wednesday _____

_____

_____

_____

_____

Thursday _____

_____

_____

_____

_____

I am Grateful for

Friday _____

_____
_____
_____
_____

Saturday _____

_____
_____
_____
_____

Sunday _____

_____
_____
_____

Strength is found within;
it can be strengthened through
the love of others.

I am Grateful for

Monday _____

_____

_____

_____

Tuesday _____

_____

_____

_____

Wednesday _____

_____

_____

_____

_____

Thursday _____

_____

_____

_____

_____

I am Grateful for

Friday _____

_____

_____

_____

Saturday _____

_____

_____

_____

_____

Sunday _____

_____

_____

_____

Gratitude
is not taking anything for granted.

I am Grateful for

Monday _____

_____

_____

_____

Tuesday _____

_____

_____

_____

Wednesday _____

_____

_____

_____

Thursday _____

_____

_____

_____

I am Grateful for

Friday _____

_____

_____

_____

Saturday _____

_____

_____

_____

_____

Sunday _____

_____

_____

_____

Love
is when your heart glows and
touches the heart of another.

I am Grateful for

Monday _____
_____
_____
_____

Tuesday _____
_____
_____
_____

Wednesday _____
_____
_____
_____

Thursday _____
_____
_____
_____

I am Grateful for

Friday _____

_____

_____

_____

_____

Saturday _____

_____

_____

_____

_____

Sunday _____

_____

_____

_____

A grateful person knows that there is goodness in each day, because each day they experience it.

I am Grateful for

Monday _____
_____
_____
_____

Tuesday _____
_____
_____
_____

Wednesday _____
_____
_____
_____
_____

Thursday _____
_____
_____
_____

I am Grateful for

Friday _____
_____
_____
_____
_____

Saturday _____
_____
_____
_____
_____

Sunday _____
_____
_____
_____

There is something new
to learn every day

I am Grateful for

Monday _____
_____
_____
_____

Tuesday _____
_____
_____
_____

Wednesday _____
_____
_____
_____
_____

Thursday _____
_____
_____
_____
_____

I am Grateful for

Friday _____

_____

_____

_____

Saturday _____

_____

_____

_____

_____

Sunday _____

_____

_____

_____

Happiness
is taking time to achieve the perfect life

balance for you.

I am Grateful for

Monday _____
_____
_____
_____

Tuesday _____
_____
_____
_____

Wednesday _____
_____
_____
_____

Thursday _____
_____
_____
_____

I am Grateful for

Friday _____

_____

_____

_____

_____

Saturday _____

_____

_____

_____

_____

Sunday _____

_____

_____

_____

When we are happy,
those who truly love us
will be happy too.

I am Grateful for

Monday _____
_____
_____
_____
_____

Tuesday _____
_____
_____
_____
_____

Wednesday _____
_____
_____
_____
_____

Thursday _____
_____
_____
_____
_____

I am Grateful for

Friday _____
_____
_____
_____

Saturday _____
_____
_____
_____
_____

Sunday _____
_____
_____
_____

Nature is the natural energy source.
Take a moment to connect and recharge
your inner core

I am Grateful for

Monday _____
_____
_____
_____

Tuesday _____
_____
_____
_____

Wednesday _____
_____
_____
_____

Thursday _____
_____
_____
_____

I am Grateful for

Friday _____

_____

_____

_____

_____

Saturday _____

_____

_____

_____

_____

Sunday _____

_____

_____

_____

We cannot often control the actions of others; but we can control how we react to them and how we let their actions impact on our life.

I am Grateful for

Monday _____
_____
_____
_____

Tuesday _____
_____
_____
_____

Wednesday _____
_____
_____
_____

Thursday _____
_____
_____
_____

I am Grateful for

Friday _____

_____

_____

_____

_____

Saturday _____

_____

_____

_____

_____

Sunday _____

_____

_____

_____

Life, Love, Inspiration, Forgiveness,
Enjoy!

I am Grateful for

Monday _____

_____

_____

_____

Tuesday _____

_____

_____

_____

Wednesday _____

_____

_____

_____

Thursday _____

_____

_____

_____

I am Grateful for

Friday _____

_____

_____

_____

_____

Saturday _____

_____

_____

_____

_____

Sunday _____

_____

_____

_____

There will be moments of sadness in life;
they will be a mere shadow when the

light of happiness shines through.

Quotes to Note

Quotes to Note

THE EXPRESSION
COLLECTION

Gratitude Journal
THE EXPRESSION COLLECTION
CREATED BY SERENITY PRESS

Attraction Journal
THE EXPRESSION COLLECTION
CREATED BY SERENITY PRESS

Intention Journal
THE EXPRESSION COLLECTION
CREATED BY SERENITY PRESS

Positivity Journal
THE EXPRESSION COLLECTION
CREATED BY SERENITY PRESS

Inspiration Journal
THE EXPRESSION COLLECTION
CREATED BY SERENITY PRESS

.WWW.SERENITYPRESS.ORG